UKULELE

CHART HITS

OF 2021-2022

ISBN 978-1-70516-101-2

HAL•LEONARD®

For all works contained herein:
Unauthorized copying, arranging, adapting, recording, internet posting, public performance,
or other distribution of the music in this publication is an infringement of copyright.
Infringers are liable under the law.

Visit Hal Leonard Online at
www.halleonard.com

World headquarters, contact:
Hal Leonard
7777 West Bluemound Road
Milwaukee, WI 53213
Email: info@halleonard.com

In Europe, contact:
Hal Leonard Europe Limited
42 Wigmore Street
Marylebone, London, W1U 2RN
Email: info@halleonardeurope.com

In Australia, contact:
Hal Leonard Australia Pty. Ltd.
4 Lentara Court
Cheltenham, Victoria, 3192 Australia
Email: info@halleonard.com.au

CONTENTS

All Too Well

Words and Music by Taylor Swift and Liz Rose

1. I walked through the door with you; the air was cold, but some-thin' 'bout it felt like home some - how. And I left my scarf there at your sis - ter's house, and you've still got it in your drawer e - ven now.

2. Oh, your

Copyright © 2012 SONGS OF UNIVERSAL, INC., TAYLOR SWIFT MUSIC, SONY MUSIC PUBLISHING (US) LLC,
WARNER-TAMERLANE PUBLISHING CORP. and LIZ ROSE MUSIC
All Rights for TAYLOR SWIFT MUSIC Administered by SONGS OF UNIVERSAL, INC.
All Rights for SONY MUSIC PUBLISHING (US) LLC Administered by
SONY MUSIC PUBLISHING (US) LLC, 424 Church Street, Suite 1200, Nashville, TN 37219
All Rights for LIZ ROSE MUSIC Administered by WARNER-TAMERLANE PUBLISHING CORP.
All Rights Reserved   Used by Permission

Chorus

'Cause there we are _ a-gain _ on that lit-tle town _ street. _ You

al-most ran _ the red _ 'cause you were look-in' o - ver at me. Wind in my hair, _

_ I was there, _ I re-mem-ber it all _ too well. _

3. Pho - to _ Yeah. _

Interlude

Bridge

May-be we got lost in _ trans-la-tion. May-be I

asked for ___ too much. But may - be this thing was a mas - ter - piece till you

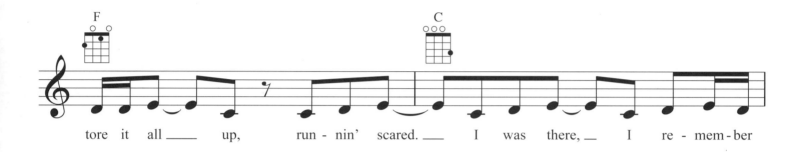

tore it all ___ up, run - nin' scared. ___ I was there, ___ I re - mem - ber

it all ___ too ___ well. ___ And you

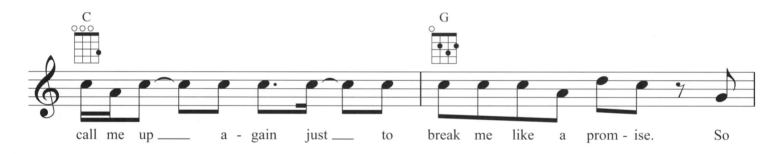

call me up ___ a - gain just ___ to break me like a prom - ise. So

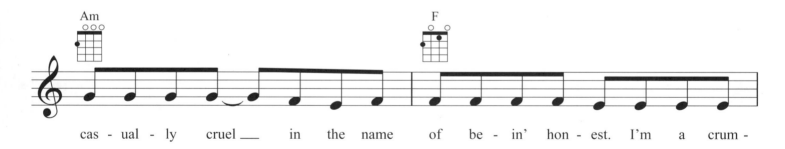

cas - ual - ly cruel ___ in the name of be - in' hon - est. I'm a crum -

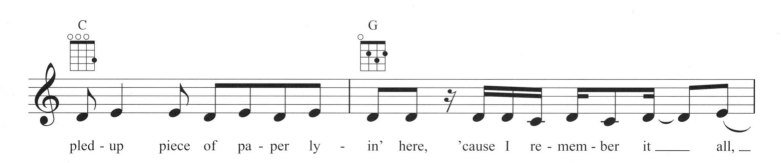

pled - up piece of pa - per ly - in' here, 'cause I re - mem - ber it ___ all, ___

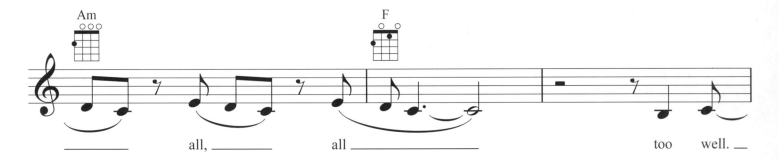

_____ all, _____ all _____ too well. __

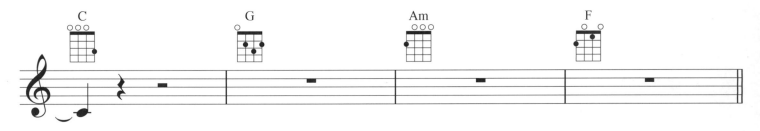

Verse

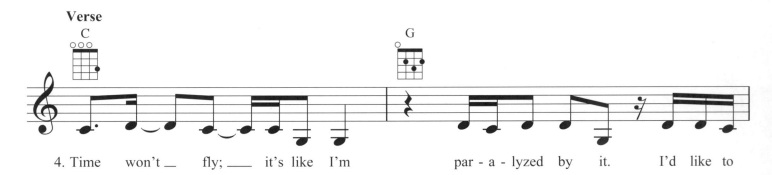

4. Time won't __ fly; __ it's like I'm par - a - lyzed by it. I'd like to

be my old self __ a - gain, but I'm still tryin' to find __ it af - ter

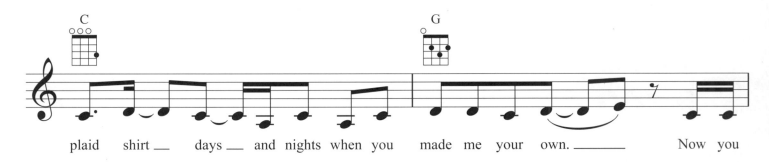

plaid shirt __ days __ and nights when you made me your own. _____ Now you

mail back my things __ and I walk home a - lone. __ But you

keep my old scarf ___ from that ver - y first ___ week ___ 'cause it re -

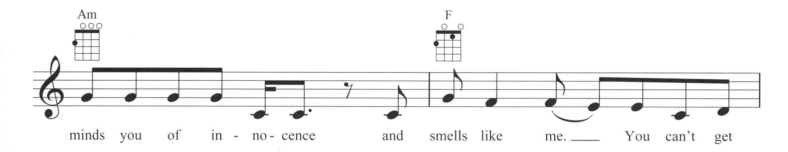

minds you of in - no - cence and smells like me. ___ You can't get

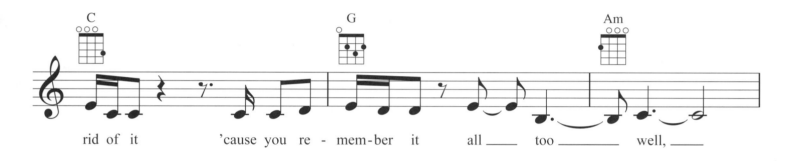

rid of it 'cause you re - mem - ber it all ___ too ___ well, ___

Chorus

yeah. ___ 'Cause there we are ___ a - gain ___ when I

loved you so, ___ back be - fore ___ you lost ___ the one real

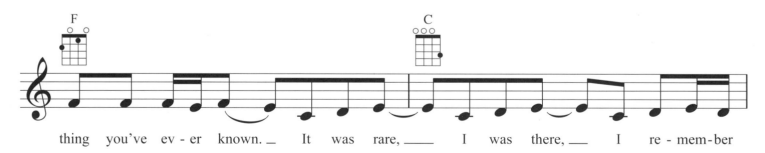

thing you've ev - er known. ___ It was rare, ___ I was there, ___ I re - mem - ber

9

Additional Lyrics

3. Photo album on the counter, your cheeks were turnin' red.
   You used to be a little kid with glasses in a twin-size bed.
   Your mother's tellin' stories 'bout you on the tee-ball team.
   You tell me 'bout your past, thinkin' your future was me.

Pre-Chorus: And I know it's long gone and there was nothin' else I could do.
   And I forget about you long enough to forget why I needed to.

Chorus: 'Cause there we are again in the middle of the night.
   We're dancin' 'round the kitchen in the refrigerator light.
   Down the stairs, I was there, I remember it all too well.

Easy on Me

Words and Music by Adele Adkins and Greg Kurstin

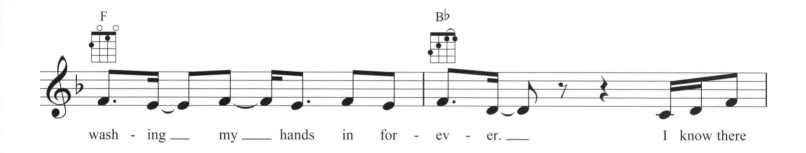

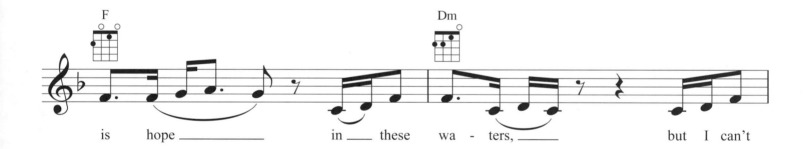

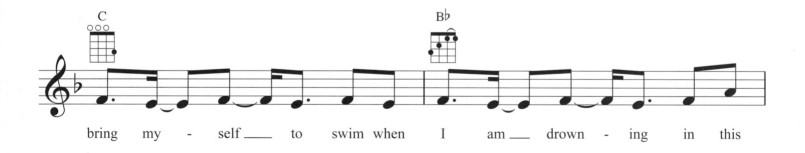

Copyright © 2021 MELTED STONE PUBLISHING LTD., EMI APRIL MUSIC INC. and KURSTIN MUSIC
All Rights for MELTED STONE PUBLISHING LTD. in the U.S. and Canada Administered by
UNIVERSAL - POLYGRAM INTERNATIONAL TUNES, INC.
All Rights for EMI APRIL MUSIC INC. and KURSTIN MUSIC Administered by
SONY MUSIC PUBLISHING (US) LLC, 424 Church Street, Suite 1200, Nashville, TN 37219
All Rights Reserved   Used by Permission

si - lence,___ ba - by. Let me in._____ Go

Chorus

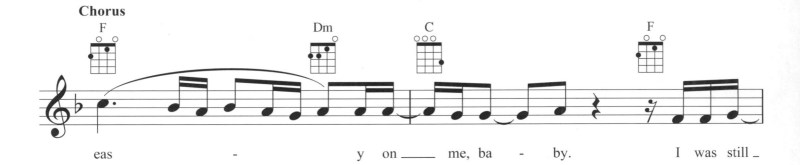

eas - y on ___ me, ba - by. I was still ___

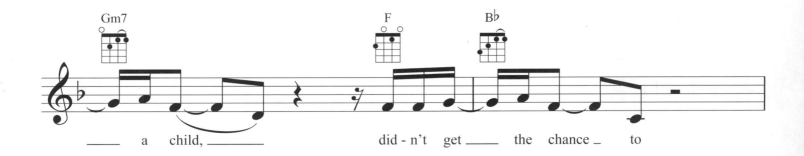

___ a child, _____ did - n't get ___ the chance ___ to

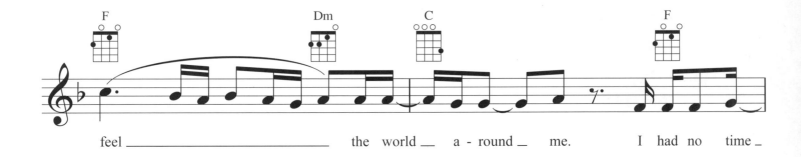

feel _____ the world ___ a - round ___ me. I had no time ___

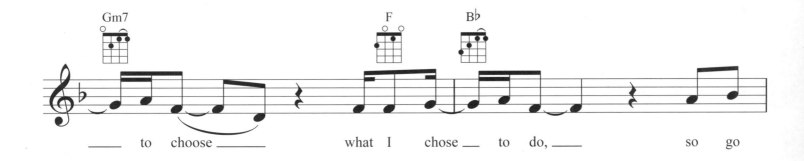

___ to choose _____ what I chose ___ to do, ___ so go

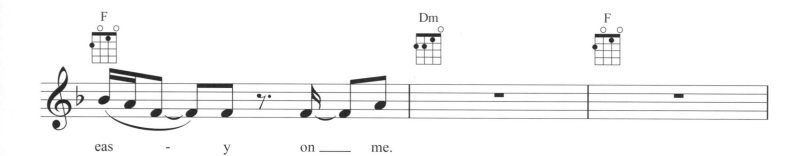

eas - y on ___ me.

Verse

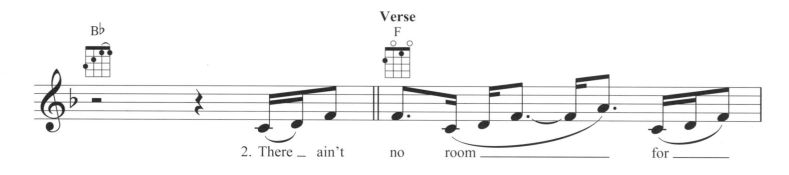

2. There _ ain't no room _____ for _____

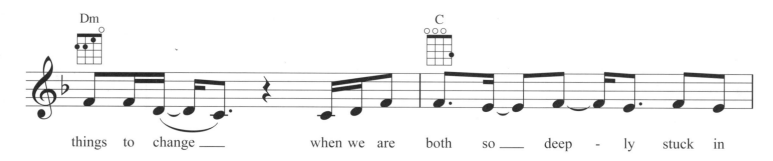

things to change ___ when we are both so ___ deep - ly stuck in

our ways. ___ You ___ can't de - ny _____ how ___ hard

I've tried. ___ I changed who I ___ was ___ to put you

both first, ___ but ___ now I give up. _____ Go

Bridge

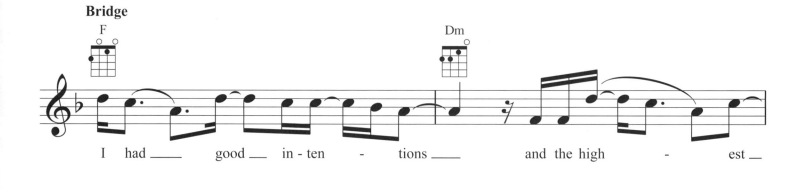

I had good in-ten-tions and the high-est

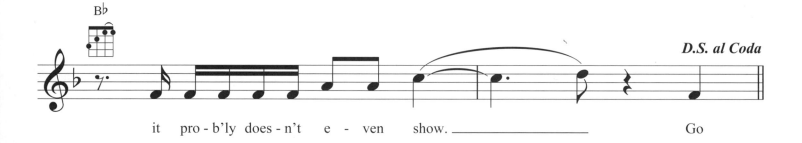

hopes, but I know right now

it pro-b'ly does-n't e-ven show. *D.S. al Coda* Go

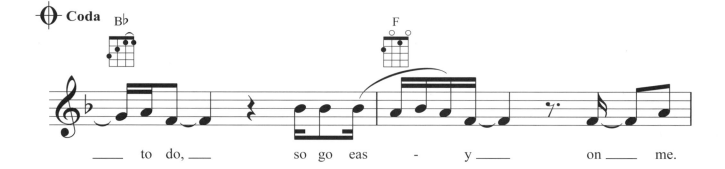

Coda

to do, so go eas-y on me.

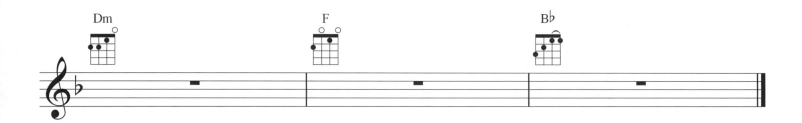

Cold Heart

(PNAU Remix)

Words and Music by Elton John, Bernard J.P. Taupin, Nicholas Littlemore, Peter Mayes, Sam Littlemore, Dean Meredith and Andrew John Meecham

Copyright © 2021 UNIVERSAL MUSIC PUBLISHING LTD., COW DOG MUSIC, INC., HST PUBLISHING LTD.,
CHENFELD LTD., UNIVERSAL MUSIC PUBLISHING PTY LTD. and BMG RIGHTS MANAGEMENT (UK) LTD.
All Rights for UNIVERSAL MUSIC PUBLISHING LTD., COW DOG MUSIC, INC. and CHENFELD LTD. in the United States
Administered by UNIVERSAL - POLYGRAM INTERNATIONAL PUBLISHING, INC.
All Rights for HST PUBLISHING LTD. and UNIVERSAL MUSIC PUBLISHING PTY LTD. in the United States
Administered by UNIVERSAL - SONGS OF POLYGRAM INTERNATIONAL, INC.
All Rights for BMG RIGHTS MANAGEMENT (UK) LTD. Administered by BMG RIGHTS MANAGEMENT (US) LLC
All Rights Reserved   Used by Permission
- Contains elements of "Sacrifice" and "Rocket Man (I Think It's Gonna Be A Long Long Time)" by Elton John and Bernie Taupin

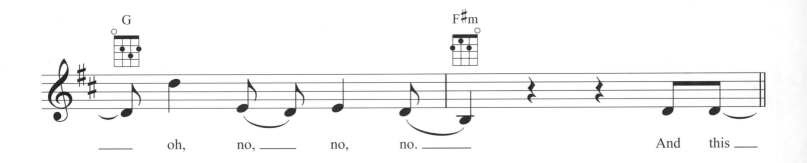

oh, ___ no, ___ no, ___ no. ___ And this ___

Bridge

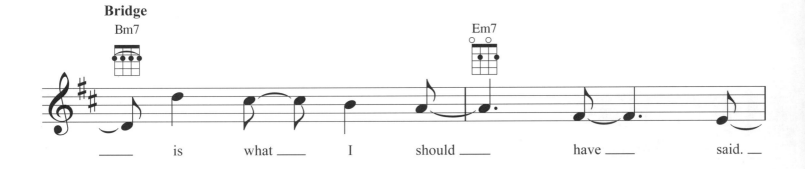

___ is what ___ I should ___ have ___ said. ___

___ Well, I thought ___ it, but ___ I kept ___

To Coda

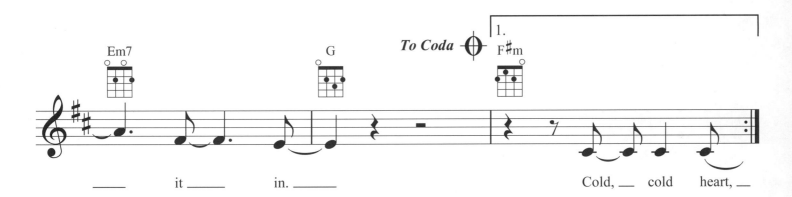

___ it ___ in. ___ Cold, ___ cold heart, ___

Pre-Chorus

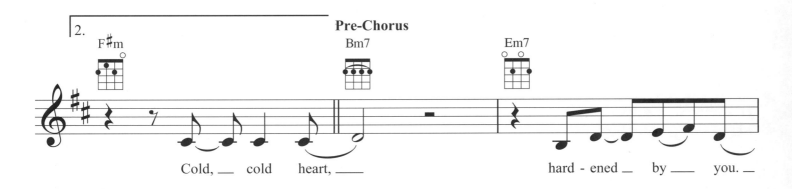

Cold, ___ cold heart, ___ hard - ened by ___ you. ___

Fancy Like

Words and Music by Walker Hayes, Josh Jenkins, Shane Stevens and Cameron Bartolini

1. My girl is bang - in', she's so low main - t'nance, don't need no
(2.) Tes - la to im - press her. My girl is

cham - pagne pop - pin' en - ter - tain - ment. Take her to
hap - py roll - in' on a Ves - pa. Don't need no

Wen - dy's, can't keep her off me. She wan - na
man - sion to get ro - manc - in'. She's su - per

dip me like them fries in her Frost - y.}
fine, __ dou - ble wide, slow __ danc - in'.}

But

Copyright © 2021 Songs Of Smack, Smack Songs LLC, Smackworks Music, Smack Blue LLC, Purplebeatz, Holy Graffiti Music,
WC Music Corp., Cameron Bartolini Music and Spark In Your Pocket
All Rights for Songs Of Smack and Smack Songs LLC Administered Worldwide by Songs Of Kobalt Music Publishing
All Rights for Smackworks Music and Smack Blue LLC Administered Worldwide by Kobalt Group Publishing
All Rights for Purplebeatz and Holy Graffiti Music Administered by Music Of MAM
All Rights for Cameron Barolini Music Administered by WC Music Corp.
All Rights for Spark In Your Pocket Administered by Me Gusta 30 Music
All Rights Reserved   Used by Permission

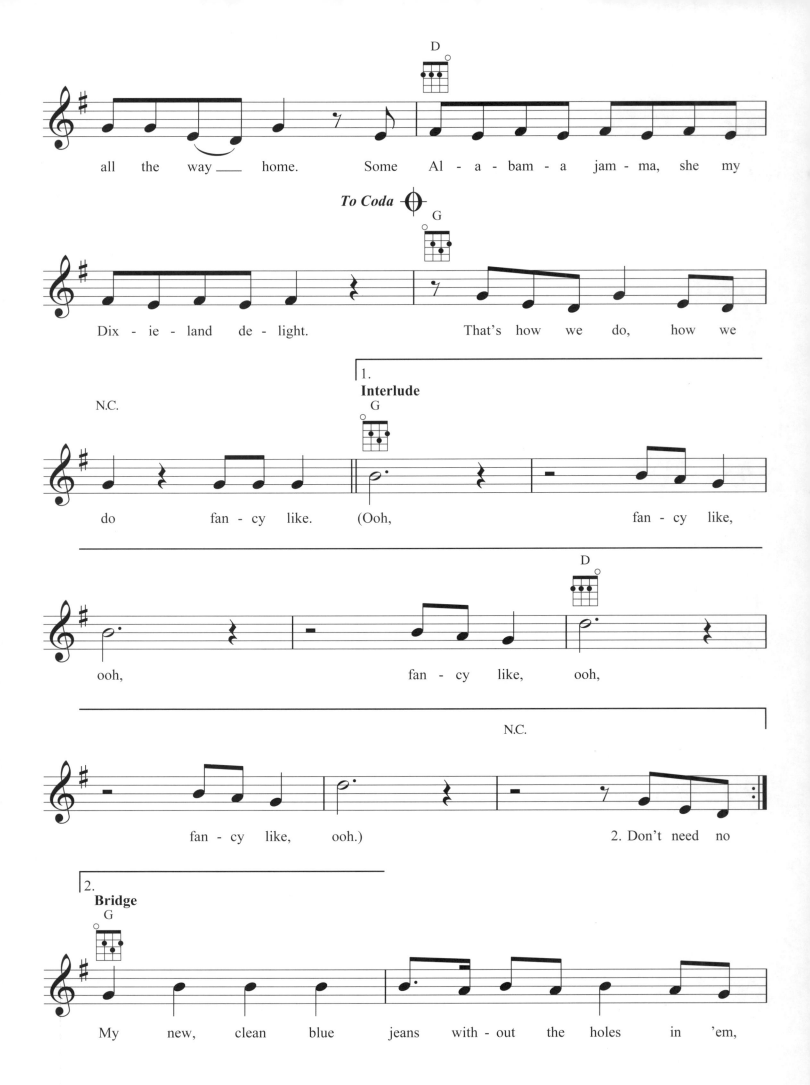

all the way ___ home. Some Al - a - bam - a jam - ma, she my

To Coda ⊕
Dix - ie - land de - light. That's how we do, how we

1.
Interlude
N.C.
do fan - cy like. (Ooh,   fan - cy like,

ooh,   fan - cy like,   ooh,

N.C.
fan - cy like,   ooh.)   2. Don't need no

2.
Bridge
G
My   new,   clean   blue   jeans   with - out   the   holes   in 'em,

coun - try kiss - es on my lips with - out Skoal in 'em.

Yeah, she's prob - 'ly gon' be keep - in' some Vic - tor - ia's Se - crets.

May - be lit - tle May - bel - line, but she don't need it in the

kitch - en light. Ra - di - o slows down, boxed wine, then her up - do

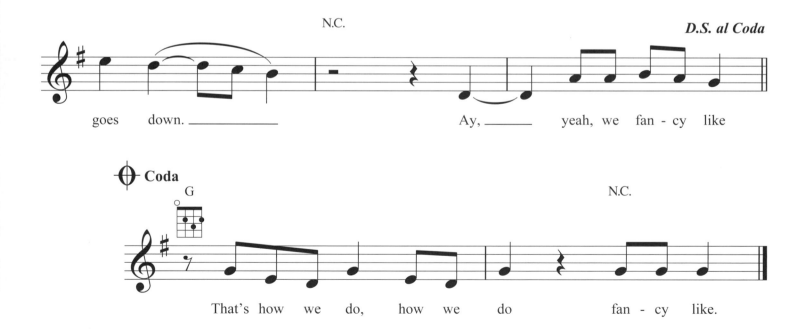

D.S. al Coda

N.C.

goes down. _____ Ay, _____ yeah, we fan - cy like

Coda

G

N.C.

That's how we do, how we do fan - cy like.

Ghost

**Words and Music by Justin Bieber, Jonathan Bellion, Jordan Johnson,
Stefan Johnson and Michael Pollack**

**Verse
Moderately, in 2**

1. Young blood thinks there's al - ways to - mor - row.
2. Young blood thinks there's al - ways to - mor - row.

I miss your touch on nights ___ when I'm hol - low.
Need more time, but time ___ can't be bor - rowed.

I know you crossed a bridge that
I'd leave it all be - hind if

I can't fol - low.)
I could fol - low.)

Since the

Copyright © 2021 UNIVERSAL MUSIC CORP., BIEBER TIME PUBLISHING, SONGS OF UNIVERSAL, INC., ART IN THE FODDER MUSIC,
BMG BUMBLEBEE, BMG PLATINUM SONGS US, SONGS OF A BEAUTIFUL MIND, SONGS OF BBMG, 1916 PUBLISHING,
HIPGNOSIS SFH I LIMITED, WARNER-TAMERLANE PUBLISHING CORP., ANTHEM STATE OF MIND and SONGS WITH A PURE TONE
All Rights for BIEBER TIME PUBLISHING Administered by UNIVERSAL MUSIC CORP.
All Rights for ART IN THE FODDER MUSIC Administered by SONGS OF UNIVERSAL, INC.
All Rights for BMG BUMBLEBEE, BMG PLATINUM SONGS US, SONGS OF A BEAUTIFUL MIND and SONGS OF BBMG
Administered by BMG RIGHTS MANAGEMENT (US) LLC
All Rights for 1916 PUBLISHING and HIPGNOSIS SFH I LIMITED Administered Worldwide by KOBALT SONGS MUSIC PUBLISHING
All Rights for ANTHEM STATE OF MIND and SONGS WITH A PURE TONE Administered by WARNER-TAMERLANE PUBLISHING CORP.
All Rights Reserved   Used by Permission

25

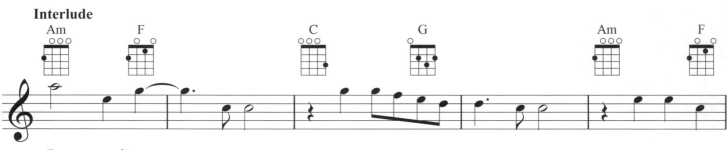

(Instrumental)

Chorus

So if I can't get close ___ to you,

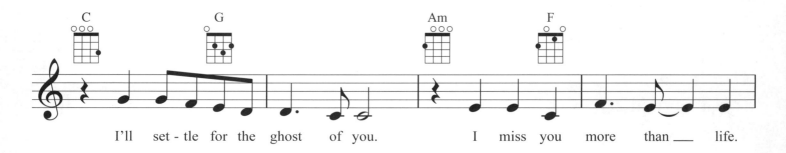

I'll set - tle for the ghost of you. I miss you more than ___ life.

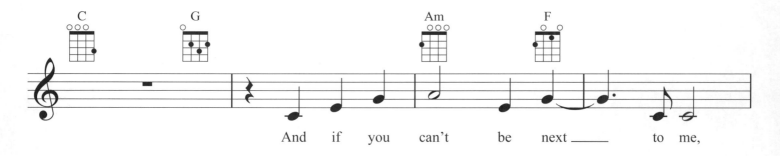

And if you can't be next ___ to me,

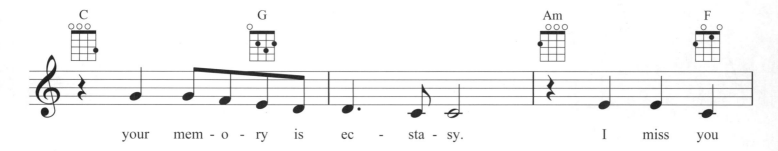

your mem - o - ry is ec - sta - sy. I miss you

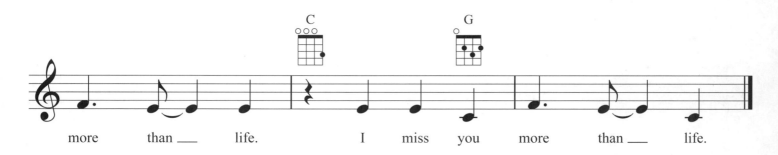

more than ___ life. I miss you more than ___ life.

Heat Waves

Words and Music by Dave Bayley

Copyright © 2020 Beggars Songs
All Rights Administered by Hipgnosis Songs Group
All Rights Reserved   Used by Permission

Verse

1. U-sual-ly I put __ some-thing on T - V __ so we nev-er think __ a-bout you and me. __

__ But to-day I see __ our re-flec-tions clear - ly in Hol-ly - wood __ lay-ing on the screen. __

__ You just need a bet-ter life than this, _____ you need some-thing I can nev - er give. _____

__ Fake wa-ter all a-cross the road, _____ it's gone now, the night has come, __ but...

Chorus

Some - times all I think a-bout is you, _____ late __ nights in the mid-dle of June. __

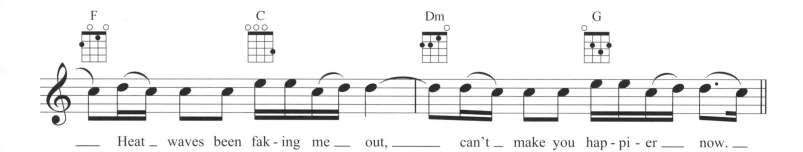

___ Heat ___ waves been fak - ing me ___ out, _____ can't ___ make you hap - pi - er ___ now. ___

Verse

2. You can't fight ___ it, you can't ___ breathe. ___ You say some - thing so lov - ing, ___ but

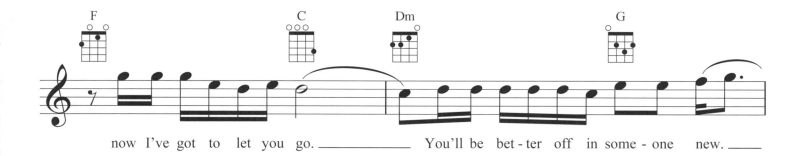

now I've got to let you go. _____ You'll be bet - ter off in some - one new. _____

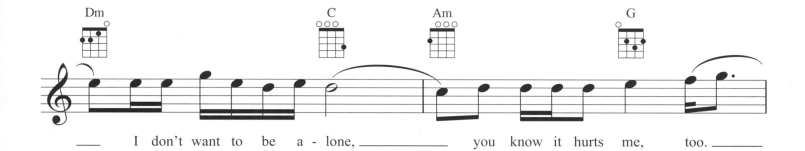

___ I don't want to be a - lone, _____ you know it hurts me, too. _____

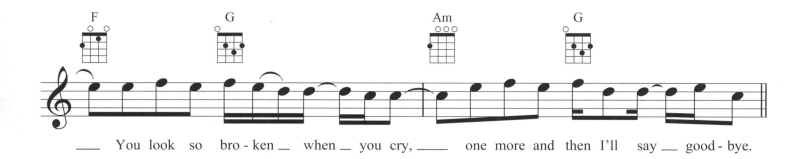

___ You look so bro - ken ___ when ___ you cry, _____ one more and then I'll say ___ good - bye.

_____ Heat _ waves been fak-ing me _ out, _____ heat _ waves been fak-ing me _ out. _____

Chorus

Some - times all I think a-bout is you, _____ late _ nights in the mid-dle of June. _

_____ Heat _ waves been fak-ing me _ out, _____ can't _ make you hap-pi-er _____ now. _

Outro

Road shim-mer, wig-gl-ing the vi-sion. Heat, heat waves, _ I'm swim-ming in a mir-ror.

Road shim-mer, wig-gl-ing the vi-sion. Heat, heat waves, _ I'm swim-ming in a mir-ror.

Happier Than Ever

Words and Music by Billie Eilish O'Connell and Finneas O'Connell

Copyright © 2020 UNIVERSAL MUSIC CORP., DRUP and LAST FRONTIER
All Rights for DRUP Administered by UNIVERSAL MUSIC CORP.
All Rights for LAST FRONTIER Administered Worldwide by KOBALT SONGS MUSIC PUBLISHING
All Rights Reserved   Used by Permission

_____ clev - er, to write my - self a let -

ter to tell me what to do. _____

Verse

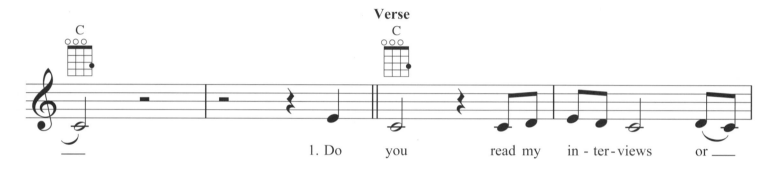

_____ 1. Do you read my in - ter - views or _____

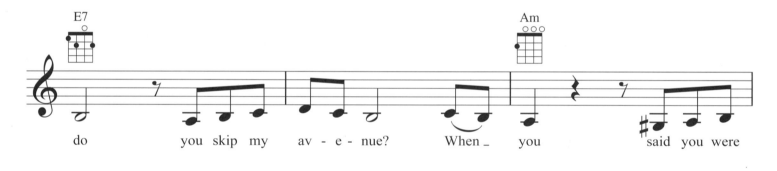

do you skip my av - e - nue? When _ you said you were

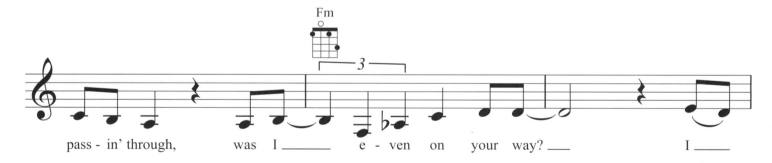

pass - in' through, was I _____ e - ven on your way? _____ I _____

knew when I asked you to be cool a - bout what I was

tell - ing you, you would do the op - po - site of what you said you'd do and I'd

___ end up more a - fraid. ___ Don't say it is - n't fair; you clear - ly

weren't a - ware that you made me mis - 'ra - ble. ___

___ So, if you real - ly wan - na know, when I'm a -

Chorus

way from you, I'm hap - pi - er than ev - - er.

Wish I could ex - plain it ___ bet - ter. I wish it was - n't

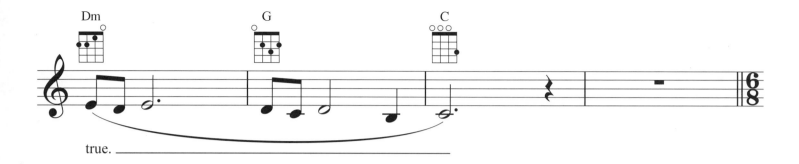

true.

Interlude
Moderate Waltz, in 2

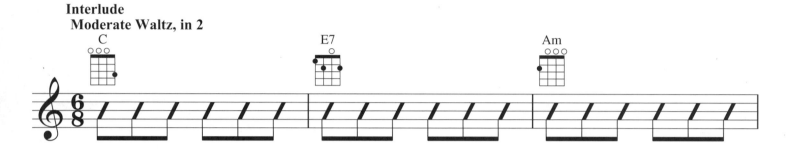

Verse

2. You call me a - gain, ___ drunk in your Benz. ___

___ Driv - in' home un - der the in - flu - ence. You scared me to death, ___

___ but I'm wast - in' my ___ breath 'cause you on - ly lis - ten to your ___ fuck in' ___

friends.
I don't re - late ___ to you.   I don't re - late ___ to you,

no. _____ 'Cause I'd nev-er treat me this shit-ty. You made me

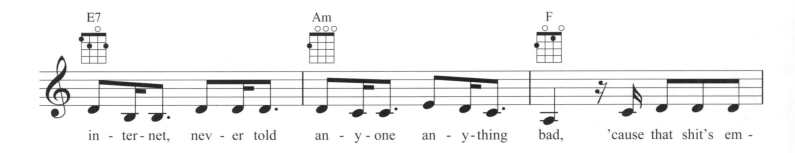

Verse

hate this _ cit-y. _ 3. And I don't talk shit a-bout you on the

in-ter-net, nev-er told an-y-one an-y-thing bad, 'cause that shit's em-

bar-rass-ing. You were my ev-'ry thing and all that you did was make me fuck-in'

sad. So don't waste the time _ I don't have, and

don't try to make _ me feel bad. I could talk a-bout ev-'ry time that you showed

If I Didn't Love You

**Words and Music by Kurt Allison, Tully Kennedy,
John Morgan and Lydia Vaughan**

Copyright © 2021 BMG Gold Songs, Makena Cove Music, BMG Platinum Songs US, Irishsonmusic,
Warner-Tamerlane Publishing Corp., Writersonthecorn Publishing and Triple Play Music
All Rights for BMG Gold Songs, Makena Cove Music, BMG Platinum Songs US and Irishsonmusic
Administered by BMG Rights Management (US) LLC
All Rights for Writersonthecorn Publishing and Triple Play Music Administered by Warner-Tamerlane Publishing Corp.
All Rights Reserved   Used by Permission

Male: Yeah, it would be eas - y not to miss you, won - der a - bout who's with you, turn the "want you" off when - ev - er I want to. If I did - n't love you, if I did - n't love you. If I did - n't love you. If I did - n't love

Female: Oh, if I did - n't love you.

Female: If I did - n't love you. If I did - n't love

Both: you. If I did - n't love you.

Outro

(Instrumental)

It'll Be Okay

Words and Music by Shawn Mendes, Scott Harris, Michael Sabath and Eddie Benjamin

Copyright © 2021 UNIVERSAL MUSIC WORKS, MENDES GMR MUSIC, SONY MUSIC PUBLISHING (US) LLC,
EMI BLACKWOOD MUSIC INC., SCOTTHARRISWRITESONGS, MODERN ARTS MELODY and SONGS BY WORK OF ART
All Rights for MENDES GMR MUSIC Administered by UNIVERSAL MUSIC WORKS
All Rights for SONY MUSIC PUBLISHING (US) LLC, EMI BLACKWOOD MUSIC INC., SCOTTHARRISWRITESONGS,
MODERN ARTS MELODY and SONGS BY WORK OF ART Administered by SONY MUSIC PUBLISHING (US) LLC,
424 Church Street, Suite 1200, Nashville, TN 37219
All Rights Reserved   Used by Permission

- ing me sick, __ but we'll heal ___ and the sun __ will __ rise.

Chorus

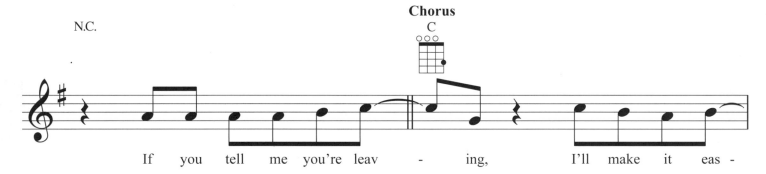

If you tell me you're leav - ing, I'll make it eas -

- y, it - 'll be o - kay.

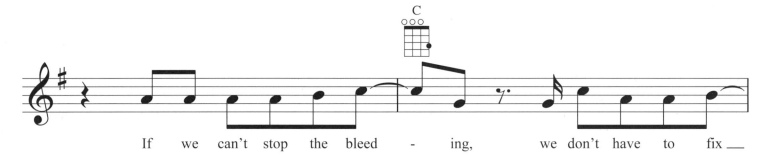

If we can't stop the bleed - ing, we don't have to fix ___

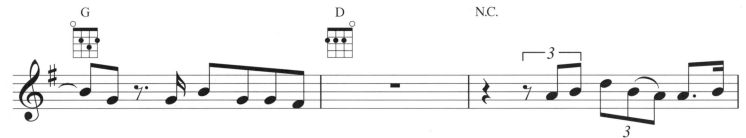

___ it, we don't have to stay. I will love you __ ei - ther

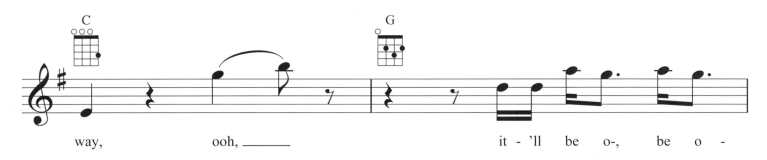

way, ooh, ___ it - 'll be o-, be o -

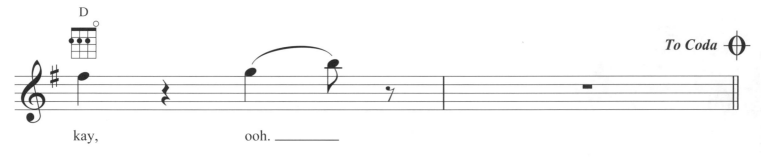

kay, ooh. _____

Verse

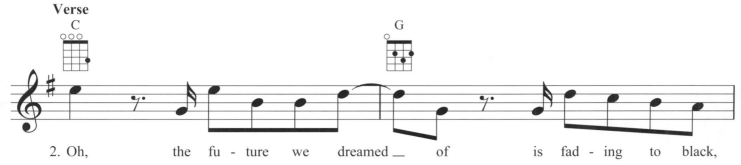

2. Oh, the fu - ture we dreamed ___ of is fad - ing to black,

oh. _____

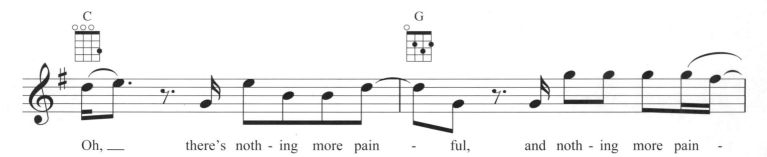

Oh, ___ there's noth - ing more pain - ful, and noth - ing more pain -

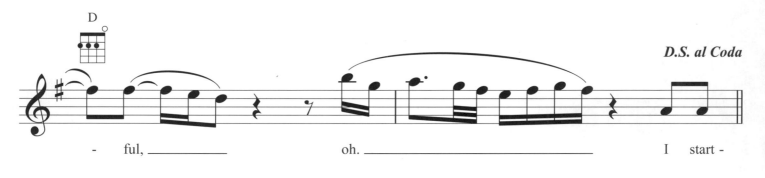

- ful, _____ oh. _____ I start -

⊕ Coda

Bridge

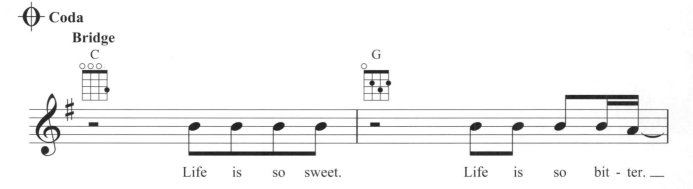

Life is so sweet. Life is so bit - ter. __

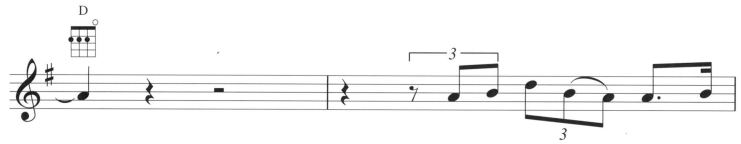

I will love you ___ ei - ther

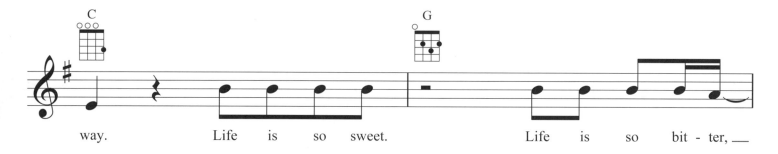

way. Life is so sweet. Life is so bit - ter, ___

___ ooh. _____

Outro

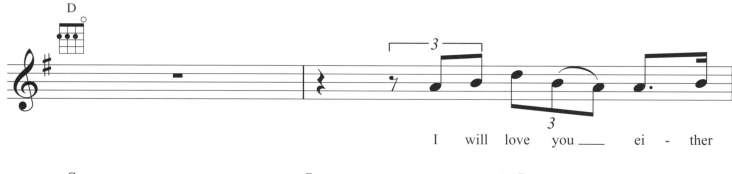

Oh, the fu - ture we dreamed ___ of is fad - ing to black.

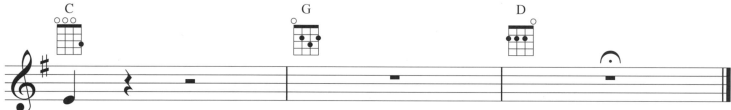

I will love you ___ ei - ther

way.

Love Again

Words and Music by Dua Lipa, Clarence Bernard Coffee, Chelcee Grimes, Stephen Kozmeniuk, Bing Crosby, Irving Wallman and Max Wartell

* Vocal written one octave higher than sung.

Copyright © 2020 TAP MUSIC PUBLISHING LTD., BEST COFFEE IN TOWN, TOMBOY MUSIC LTD., SILVER FOX MUSIC LTD.,
EMI MUSIC PUBLISHING LTD., NYANKINGMUSIC and WC MUSIC CORP.
All Rights for TAP MUSIC PUBLISHING LTD. Administered by UNIVERSAL - POLYGRAM INTERNATIONAL PUBLISHING, INC.
All Rights for BEST COFFEE IN TOWN, TOMBOY MUSIC LTD. and SILVER FOX MUSIC LTD.
Administered by KOBALT SONGS MUSIC PUBLISHING
All Rights for EMI MUSIC PUBLISHING LTD. and NYANKINGMUSIC Administered by SONY MUSIC PUBLISHING (US) LLC,
424 Church Street, Suite 1200, Nashville, TN 37219
All Rights Reserved   Used by Permission

⊕ **Coda**   **Bridge**

I can't be-lieve, I can't be-

lieve I fi-nal-ly found some-one. I'll sink my teeth in dis-be-

lief 'cause you're the one that I want. I can't be-lieve, I can't be-

lieve I'm not a-fraid an-y-more, but god-damn, you got me in love a-gain. _

Verse

4. I nev-er thought that I would

find a way out. _   I nev-er thought I'd hear my heart beat so loud. _

Em   D7

I can't be - lieve there's some - thing left in my chest ___ an - y - more,

Em   Cmaj7   Am   N.C.

but god - damn,   you got me in love a - gain. ___

Em   C   Am   D   Em   C

___

Bridge

Am   D   Em   C

I can't be - lieve, I can't be -

Am   D   Em   C

lieve I fi - nal - ly found some - one.   I'll sink my teeth in dis - be -

Am   D   Em   C

lief 'cause you're the one that I want.   I can't be - lieve there's some - thing

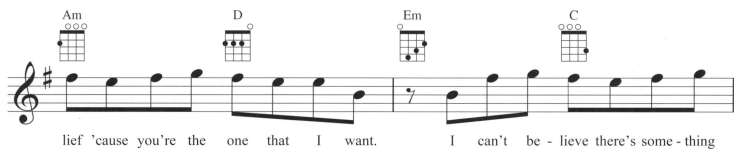

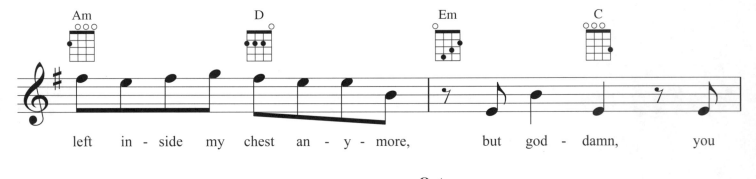

left in - side my chest an - y - more, but god - damn, you

Outro

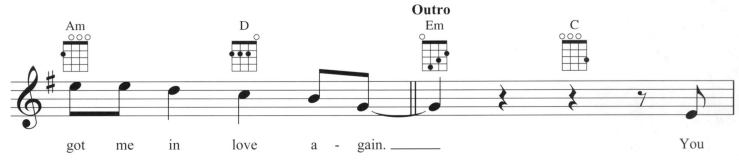

got me in love a - gain. _____ You

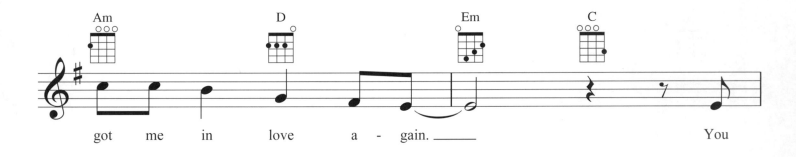

got me in love a - gain. _____ You

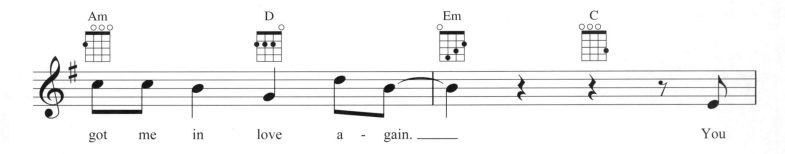

got me in love a - gain. _____ You

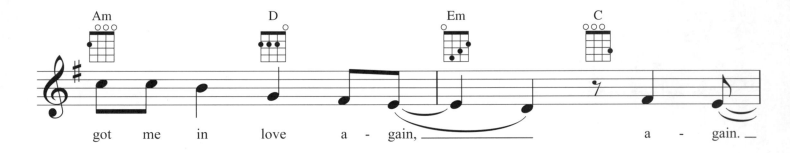

got me in love a - gain, _____ a - gain. _

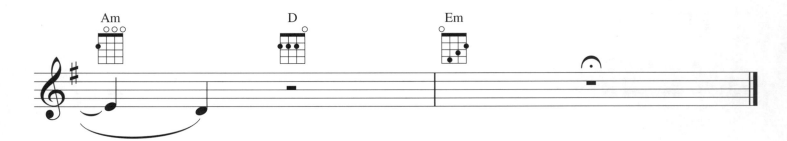

Smokin' Out the Window

Words and Music by Peter Gene Hernandez, Dernst Emile and Anderson .Paak

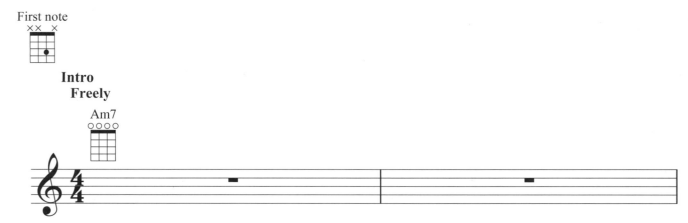

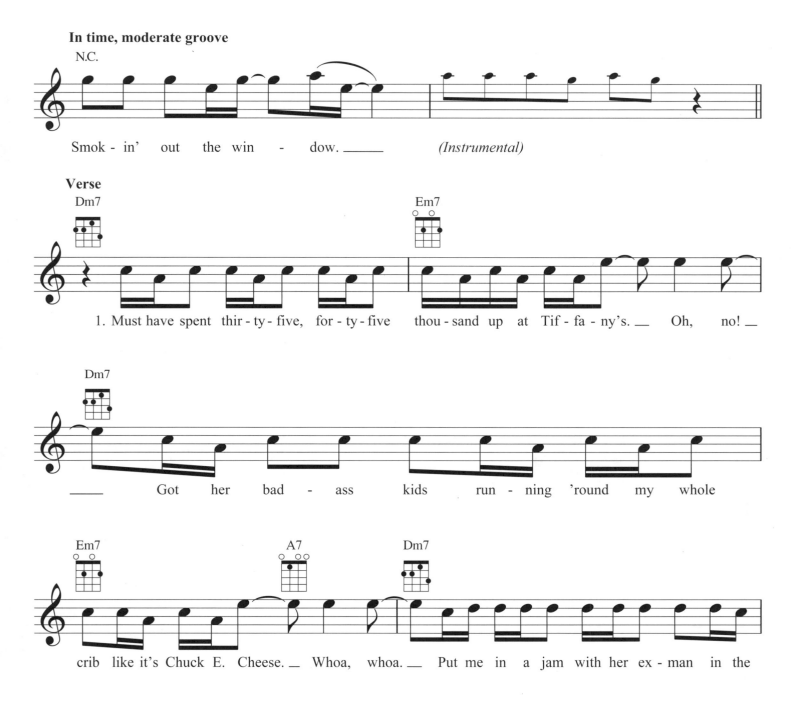

(Spoken:) "Wait a minute, this love started out so timid and so sweet. But now she got me...

Smok - in' out the win - dow. _____ (Instrumental)

1. Must have spent thir - ty - five, for - ty - five thou - sand up at Tif - fa - ny's. _ Oh, no! _

_____ Got her bad - ass kids run - ning 'round my whole

crib like it's Chuck E. Cheese. _ Whoa, whoa. _ Put me in a jam with her ex - man in the

Copyright © 2021 BMG Onyx, Mars Force Music, DII Music LLC, Warner Geo Met Ric Music,
Hard Workin' Black Folks GMR Finder Pub Designee and Khlex Dream
All Rights for BMG Onyx, Mars Force Music and DII Music LLC Administered by BMG Rights Management (US) LLC
All Rights for Hard Workin' Black Folks GMR Finder Pub Designee and Khlex Dream Administered by Warner Geo Met Ric Music
All Rights Reserved   Used by Permission

U. F. ___ C. ___ Can't be-lieve ___ it, I'm in dis-be-lief. ___
(Can't be-lieve ___ it.)

Pre-Chorus

___ This bitch got me pay-ing her rent, pay-ing for trips, dia-monds on her

neck, dia-monds on her wrist. And here I am all a - lone, ___

___ (All a - lone.) ___ I'm so cold, ___ I'm so cold. ___ You got ___ me out ___ here:

Chorus

Smok - in' out the win - dow, ___ sing - ing, "How ___

___ could she do this to me?" (How could she do this to me?) Oh, I

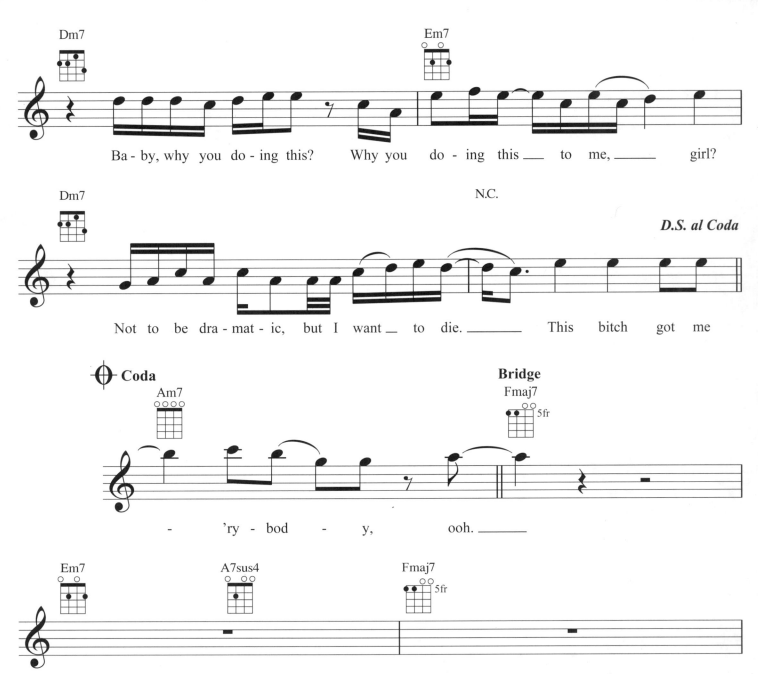

Ba - by, why you do - ing this? Why you do - ing this __ to me, _____ girl?

D.S. al Coda

Not to be dra - mat - ic, but I want __ to die. _____ This bitch got me

Coda

- 'ry - bod - y, ooh. _____

Bridge

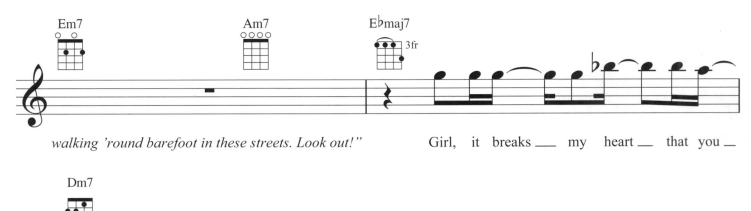

(Spoken:) "Look here, baby, I hope you found whatever it is that you need. But I also hope that your trifling ass is

walking 'round barefoot in these streets. Look out!" Girl, it breaks __ my heart __ that you __

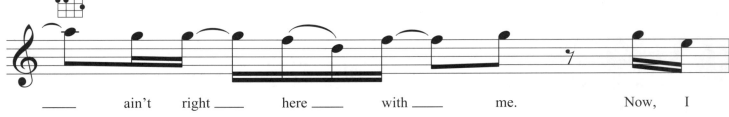

_____ ain't right __ here __ with __ me. Now, I

Chorus

got to give you back (got to give you back) to the cit-

-y. ___ Oh, ___ you got ___ me: Smok-in' out the win - dow, ___

sing-ing, "How ___ could she do this to me?'

Oh, I had thought that girl be-longed to on-

-ly me. ___ But I was wrong, ___ 'cause she be-longed to ev-

-'ry-bod-y, ev-'ry-bod-y. Ooh. ___

My Universe

Words and Music by Chris Martin, Will Champion, Jon Buckland, Guy Berryman, Max Martin,
Ho-seok Jung, Nam-joon Kim, Yoon-gi Min, Oscar Holter and Bill Rahko

First note

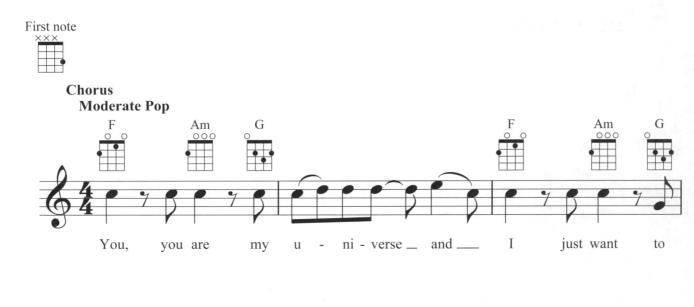

Chorus
Moderate Pop

You, you are my u - ni - verse _ and _ I just want to

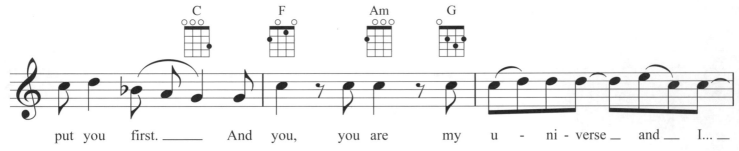

put you first. _____ And you, you are my u - ni - verse _ and _ I... _

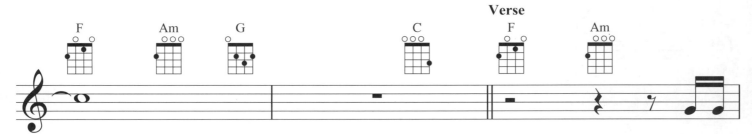

Verse

_____ 1. In the

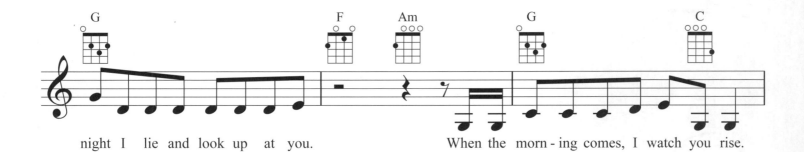

night I lie and look up at you. When the morn - ing comes, I watch you rise.

Copyright © 2021 by Universal Music Publishing MGB Ltd., MXM, Sony Music Publishing (US) LLC, Hybe Co. Ltd.,
WC Music Corp., Songs Of Wolf Cousins and Rahksongs
All Rights for Universal Music Publishing MGB Ltd. Sub-Published by Universal Music - MGB Songs in the USA
All Rights for MXM Administered Worldwide by Kobalt Songs Music Publishing
All Rights for Sony Music Publishing (US) LLC and Hybe Co. Ltd. Administered by Sony Music Publishing (US) LLC,
424 Church Street, Suite 1200, Nashville, TN 37219
All Rights for Songs Of Wolf Cousins Administered by WC Music Corp.
All Rights Reserved   Used by Permission

There's a par - a - dise they could - n't cap - ture,   that bright in -

Pre-Chorus

fin - i - ty ___ in - side your eyes. *Maeil bam ne - ge ___ na - ra - ga kku -

mi - ran geos - do i - jeun chae na u - seum - yeo neo - reul man - na.

𝄇 Chorus

Nev - er - end - ing for - ev - er, ba - by.   You,   you are   my

u - ni - verse ___ and ___ I   just want   to put you first. ___

You,   you are   my   u - ni - verse ___ and ___   you

Romanization of Korean lyrics.

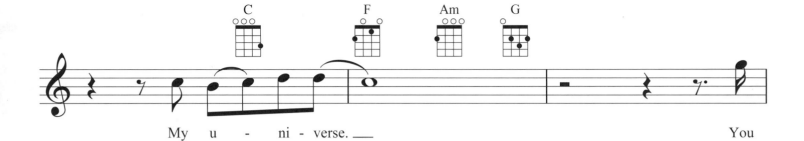

My u – ni - verse. ___ You

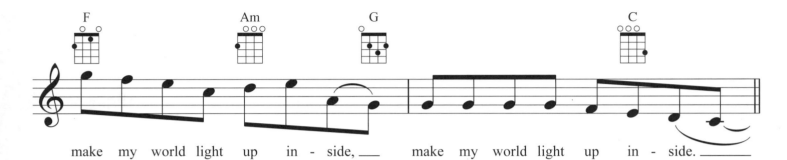

make my world light up in - side, ___ make my world light up in - side. _____

Bridge

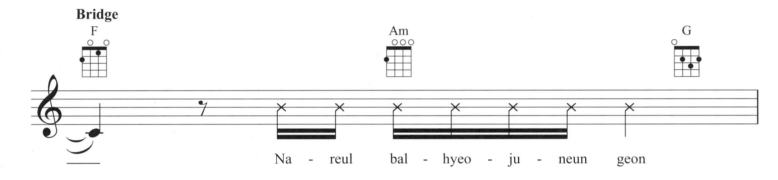

___ Na – reul bal – hyeo – ju – neun geon

neo – ran sa – ran – geu – ro su no – ha – jin byeol

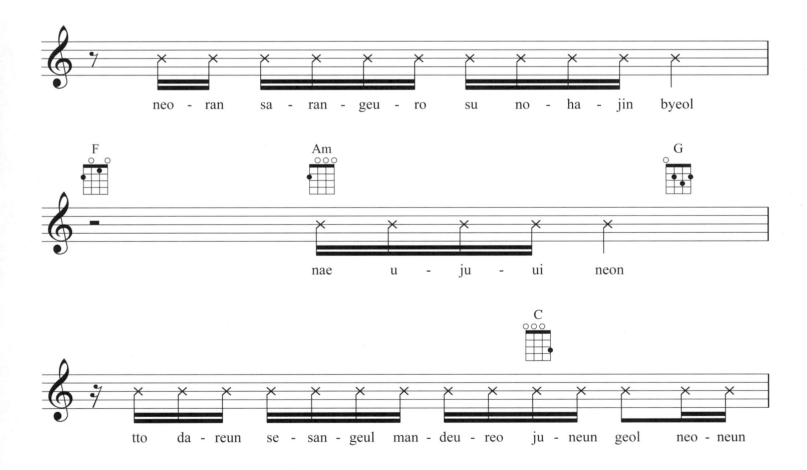

nae u – ju – ui neon

tto da – reun se – san – geul man – deu – reo ju – neun geol neo – neun

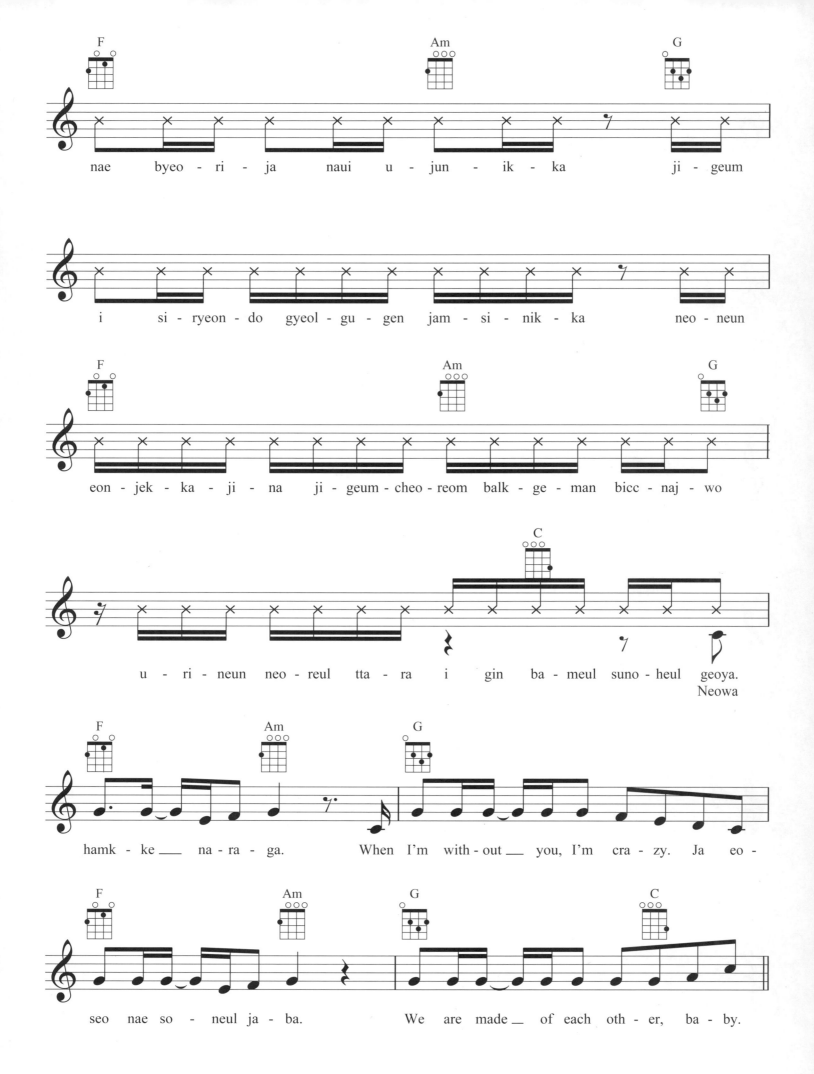

nae byeo - ri - ja naui u - jun - ik - ka ji - geum

i si - ryeon - do gyeol - gu - gen jam - si - nik - ka neo - neun

eon - jek - ka - ji - na ji - geum - cheo - reom balk - ge - man bicc - naj - wo

u - ri - neun neo - reul tta - ra i gin ba - meul suno - heul geoya.
Neowa

hamk - ke ___ na - ra - ga. When I'm with - out ___ you, I'm cra - zy. Ja eo -

seo nae so - neul ja - ba. We are made ___ of each oth - er, ba - by.

Permission to Dance

Words and Music by Ed Sheeran, Johnny McDaid, Steve Mac and Jenna Andrews

Copyright © 2021 Sony Music Publishing (UK) Ltd., Sony Music Publishing (US) LLC, Rokstone Music,
WC Music Corp. and Leaha Music Pub Designee
All Rights on behalf of Sony Music Publishing (US) LLC
Administered by Sony Music Publishing (US) LLC, 424 Church Street, Suite 1200, Nashville, TN 37219
All Rights on behalf of Rokstone Music Administered by Universal - PolyGram International Publishing, Inc.
All Rights on behalf of Leaha Music Pub Designee Administered by WC Music Corp.
International Copyright Secured   All Rights Reserved

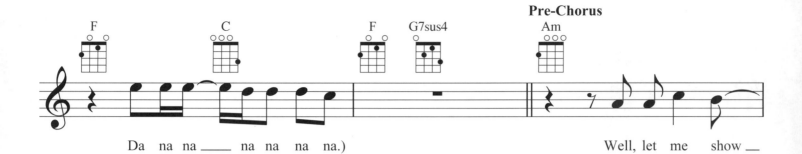

Da na na ___ na na na na.)   Well, let me show ___

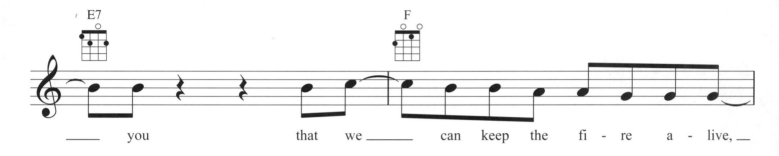

___ you   that we ___ can keep the fi - re a - live, ___

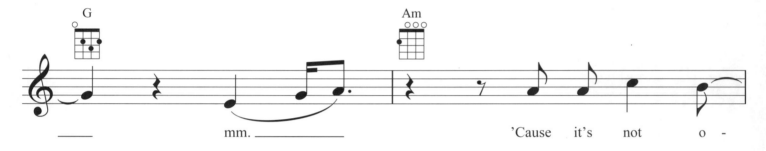

___   mm. ___   'Cause it's not o -

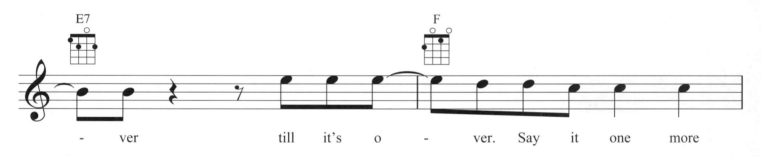

- ver   till it's o - ver. Say it one more

Chorus

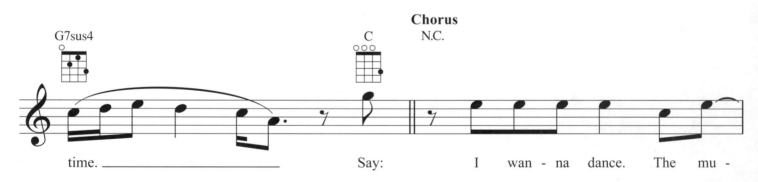

time. ___   Say: I wan - na dance. The mu -

- sic's got me go - ing, ain't noth - ing that can stop how we move. ___

Shivers

Words and Music by Ed Sheeran, Johnny McDaid, Steve Mac and Kal Lavelle

Copyright © 2021 Sony Music Publishing (UK) Limited, Sony Music Publishing (US) LLC and Rokstone Music
All Rights on behalf of Sony Music Publishing (UK) Limited and Sony Music Publishing (US) LLC
Administered by Sony Music Publishing (US) LLC, 424 Church Street, Suite 1200, Nashville, TN 37219
All Rights on behalf of Rokstone Music Administered by Universal - PolyGram International Publishing, Inc.
International Copyright Secured   All Rights Reserved

Take My Breath

Words and Music by Abel Tesfaye, Max Martin, Oscar Holter and Ahmad Balshe

Copyright © 2021 KMR Music Royalties II SCSp, MXM, WC Music Corp.,
Songs Of Wolf Cousins and Bota Music Publishing LLC Pub Designee
All Rights for KMR Music Royalties II SCSp and MXM Administered Worldwide by Kobalt Songs Music Publishing
All Rights for Songs Of Wolf Cousins and Bota Music Publishing LLC Pub Designee Administered by WC Music Corp.
All Rights Reserved   Used by Permission

You're of - fer - ing ___ your - self to me ___ like sac - ri - fice.

You said you do ___ this all the ___ time. ___

Tell me you love ___ me if I bring ___ you to the light.

Pre-Chorus

It's like a dream, what she feels ___ with ___ me. ___ She loves to

be on the edge. ___ Her fan - ta - sy is o - kay ___

___ with ___ me. ___ Then sud - den - ly, ba - by says: ___

_____ life. _____ Girl, I don't want _____ to be the one _____

_____ who pays the price. Ooh, _____ it's like a

dream, what she feels _____ with _____ me. _____ She loves to be on the edge. _____

_____ Her fan - ta - sy is o - kay _____ with _____ me. _____ Then sud - den -

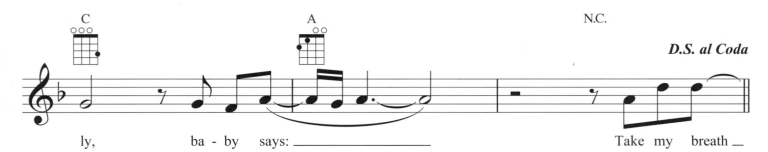

ly, ba - by says: _____ Take my breath _____

D.S. al Coda

Interlude

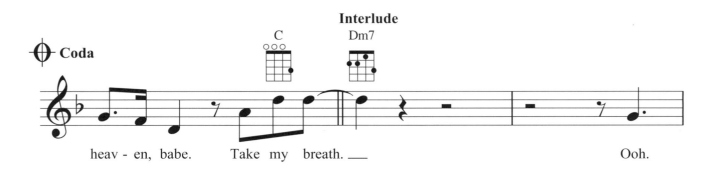

heav - en, babe. Take my breath. _____ Ooh.

Oh. _____

And they'll see ___ me. ___

Ooh, _____ ooh. _____

Bridge

Oh, _____ oh. _____ Oh, _____

oh. _____ Oh, _____ oh. _____

Chorus

Oh. _____ Take my breath ___ a - way _

We Don't Talk About Bruno

from ENCANTO
Music and Lyrics by Lin-Manuel Miranda

© 2021 Walt Disney Music Company
All Rights Reserved. Used by Permission.

Verse

2. Grew to live in fear of Bru - no stut - ter - ing or stum - bling,

I can al - ways hear him sort of mut - ter - ing and mum - bling.

I as - so - ci - ate him with the sound of fall - ing sand, ch ch ch

It's a heav - y lift, with a gift so hum - bling,

Al - ways left A - bue - la and the fam - i - ly fum - bling,

Grap - pl - ing with proph - e - cies they could - n't un - der -

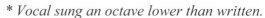
Vocal sung an octave lower than written.

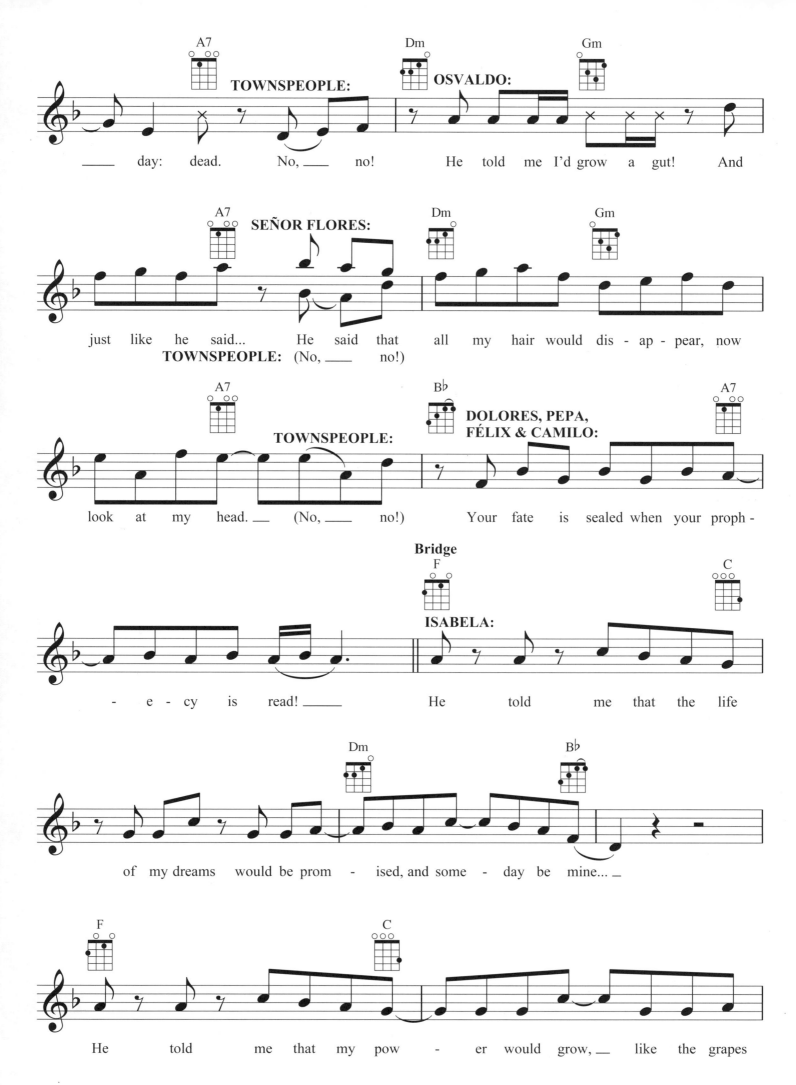

that   thrive ___ on the vine... ___ *Ó - ye,* Ma - ria - no's on his

ABUELA ALMA:

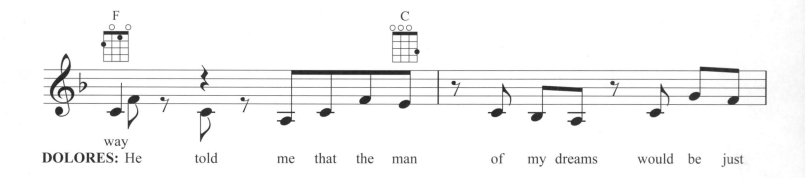

way
DOLORES: He   told   me   that   the   man   of   my   dreams   would   be   just

out   of   reach,   be - trothed   to   an - oth - er...

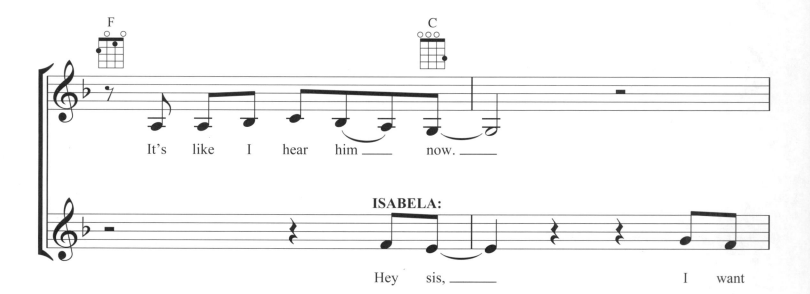

It's   like   I   hear   him ___ now. ___

ISABELA:

Hey   sis, ___   I   want

It's like I can hear him now, ___ I can hear him now!

not a sound ___ out of you... ___

Interlude

MIRABEL: Um, Bru - no... Yeah, a - bout that Bru - no... I

real - ly need to know a - bout Bru - no... Gim - me the

truth and the whole truth, Bru - no! ___ CAMILO: Is - a -

bel - a, your boy - friend's here. JULIETA & PEPA: Time for din - ner! CAMILO: A

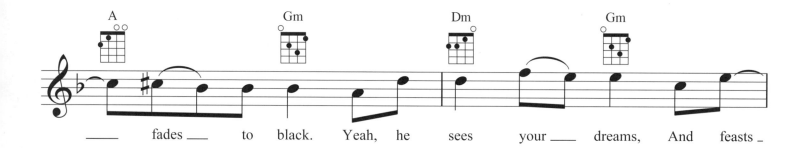

fades ___ to black. Yeah, he sees your ___ dreams, And feasts _

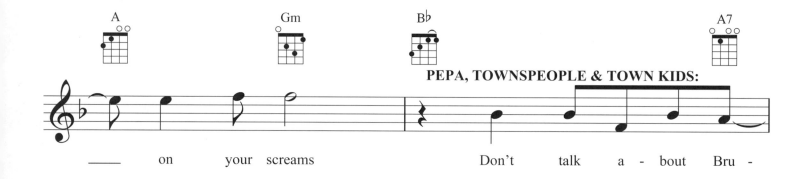

___ on your screams

PEPA, TOWNSPEOPLE & TOWN KIDS:

Don't talk a - bout Bru -

\- no, ___ no! ___

Not a word a - bout Bru -

MIRABEL:

Why did I talk a - bout Bru - no?! I

\- no! _____

nev - er should - a brought up Bru - no!

You Should Probably Leave

Words and Music by Chris Stapleton, Chris DuBois and Ashley Gorley

1. I know it ain't __ all that late, __ but you should prob-a-bly leave. __
2. There's still __ time __ for you to fin-ish your wine, __ then you should prob-a-bly leave. __

And I rec-og-nize __ that
And it's hard to re-sist. __ Al-

look in your eyes. __ Yeah, you should prob-a-bly leave. __
right, just one kiss, __ then you should prob-a-bly leave. __

Chorus

'Cause I know you and you know me, and we __

© 2011, 2012, 2020, 2021 WC MUSIC CORP., SONGS OF SOUTHSIDE INDEPENDENT MUSIC PUBLISHING,
SPIRIT TWO NASHVILLE, SEA GAYLE PUB HOUSE MUSIC and LE SEEK C'EST CHIC
All Rights for SONGS OF SOUTHSIDE INDEPENDENT MUSIC PUBLISHING Administered by WC MUSIC CORP.
All Rights for SEA GAYLE PUB HOUSE MUSIC Administered by CLEARBOX RIGHTS
All Rights for LE SEEK C'EST CHIC Administered Worldwide by KOBALT SONGS MUSIC PUBLISHING
All Rights Reserved   Used by Permission

____ both know _ where this is gon-na lead. {(1., 2.) You want me to say ___ that I
(D.S.) I want you to stay, _ but you'll

want you to stay, ___ so you should prob-a-bly leave. ___
prob-a-bly say ___ that you should prob-a-bly leave. ___

To Coda ⊕ | 1.

Yeah, you should prob-a-bly leave. _____
Yeah, you should prob-a-bly leave. _____

| 2. **Bridge**

Like a dev - il on my shoul-der, you keep whis-per-in' in my

ear. _____ And it's get - tin' kind-a hard for me

to do the right thing here. I wan-na do ___

Stay

Words and Music by Justin Bieber, Blake Slatkin, Omer Fedi, Charlie Puth, Charlton Howard,
Magnus Holberg, Michael Mule, Issac De Boni and Subhaan Rahman

Chorus
Moderate Synth Pop

I do the same thing I told you that I nev-er would. I told you I changed, e-ven when I knew I nev-er could. I know that I can't find no-bod-y else as good as you. I need you to stay, need you to stay, hey.

Copyright © 2021 UNIVERSAL MUSIC CORP., BIEBER TIME PUBLISHING, SONGS OF UNIVERSAL, INC.,
BACK HAIR MUSIC PUBLISHING, TWO HANDS AND A BIT PUBLISHING, ELECTRIC FEEL MUSIC, OMER FEDI MUSIC,
ARTIST 101 PUBLISHING GROUP, CHARLIE PUTH MUSIC PUBLISHING, SONY MUSIC PUBLISHING (US) LLC,
MAGNUS HOLBERG PUBLISHING DESIGNEE, CONCORD COPYRIGHTS o/b/o THESE ARE PULSE SONGS, MJM87 PUBLISHING,
FNZ PUBLISHING and SUBHAAN RAHMAN PUBLISHING DESIGNEE
All Rights for BIEBER TIME PUBLISHING Administered by UNIVERSAL MUSIC CORP.
All Rights for BACK HAIR MUSIC PUBLISHING, TWO HANDS AND A BIT PUBLISHING, ELECTRIC FEEL MUSIC and OMER FEDI MUSIC
Administered by SONGS OF UNIVERSAL, INC.
All Rights for ARTIST 101 PUBLISHING GROUP and CHARLIE PUTH MUSIC PUBLISHING
Administered Worldwide by SONGS OF KOBALT MUSIC PUBLISHING
All Rights for SONY MUSIC PUBLISHING (US) LLC Administered by SONY MUSIC PUBLISHING (US) LLC,
424 Church Street, Suite 1200, Nashville, TN 37219
All Rights for MAGNUS HOLBERG PUBLISHING DESIGNEE Administered by WC MUSIC CORP.
All Rights for CONCORD COPYRIGHTS o/b/o THESE ARE PULSE SONGS, MJM87 PUBLISHING and FNZ PUBLISHING
Administered by CONCORD MUSIC PUBLISHING
All Rights Reserved   Used by Permission

Verse

1. I get drunk, wake _ up, I'm wast - ed. Still, I real - ize the time _ that I wast - ed

here. I feel like you can't _ feel the way I feel.
I'll be fucked up if you can't be right _ here.

Pre-Chorus

Oh, _____ whoa, _ oh, _____ whoa, _

oh, _____ whoa. _ I'll be fucked up if you can't be right _ here.

Chorus

I do the same _ thing I told you that I nev - er would. I

told you I changed, _ e - ven when I knew I nev - er could. I

92

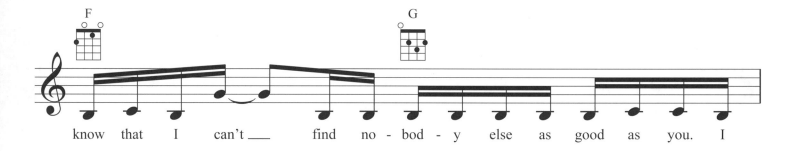

know that I can't ___ find no-bod-y else as good as you. I

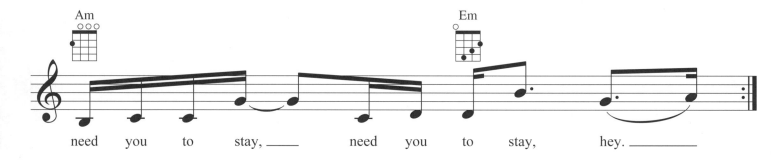

need you to stay, ___ need you to stay, hey. ___

Verse

N.C.

2. When I'm a-way from you, I miss your touch.

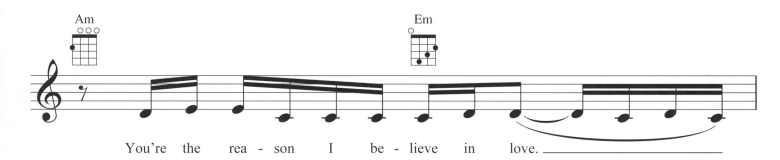

You're the rea-son I be-lieve in love. ___

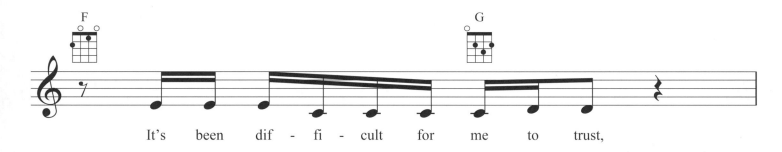

It's been dif-fi-cult for me to trust,

and I'm a-fraid that I'm a fuck it up. ___

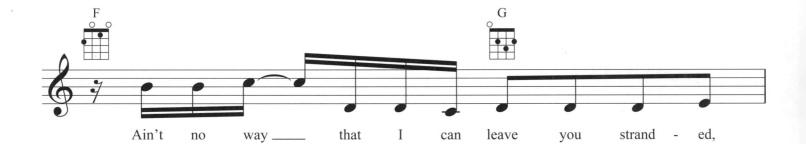

Ain't no way ___ that I can leave you strand - ed,

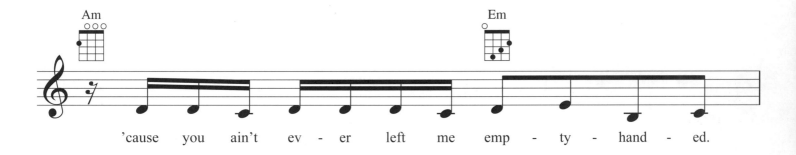

'cause you ain't ev - er left me emp - ty - hand - ed.

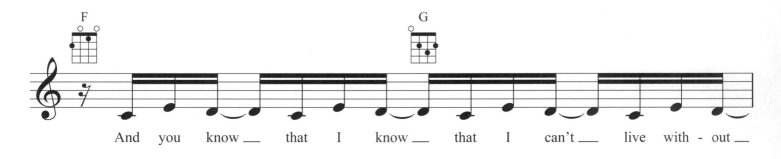

And you know ___ that I know ___ that I can't ___ live with - out ___

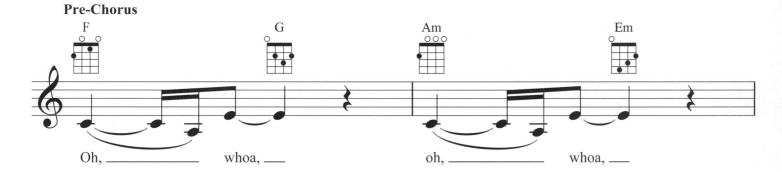

___ you, so ba - by, stay. ___

Pre-Chorus

Oh, _____ whoa, ___ oh, _____ whoa, ___

oh, _____ whoa. ___ I'll be fucked up if you can't be right ___ here.

Chorus

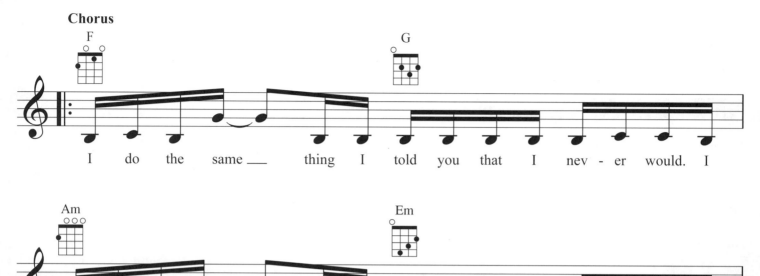

I do the same ___ thing I told you that I nev-er would. I

told you I changed, ___ e-ven when I knew I nev-er could. I

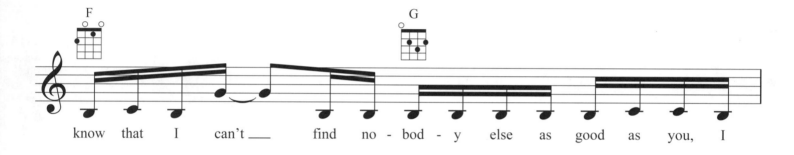

know that I can't ___ find no-bod-y else as good as you, I

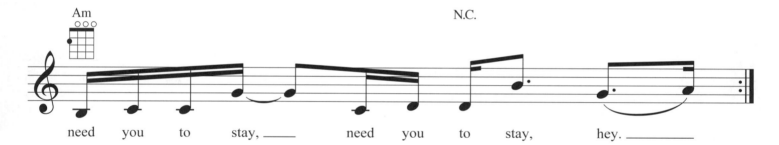

need you to stay, ___ need you to stay, hey. ___

Outro

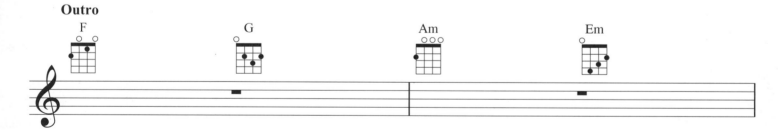

I need you to stay, ___ need you to stay, hey. ___

Ukulele Artist Songbooks

The Beatles for Fingerstyle Ukulele

arr. Fred Sokolow

25 favorite songs: Across the Universe • Can't Buy Me Love • Eight Days a Week • Here Comes the Sun • Hey Jude • Lucy in the Sky with Diamonds • Yesterday • You've Got to Hide Your Love Away • and more.

00124415 .... $19.99

Billie Eilish for Ukulele

17 Eilish songs in standard G-C-E-A tuning for ukulele: Bad Guy • 8 • Everything I Wanted • Lovely • No Time to Die • Ocean Eyes • Party Favor • Wish You Were Gay • and more.

00345575 .... $15.99

The Doors for Ukulele

Now you can strum along to 15 Doors classics on the ukulele: Break on Through (To the Other Side) • Hello, I Love You • L.A. Woman • Light My Fire • Love Her Madly • People Are Strange • Riders on the Storm • Waiting for the Sun • more.

00345914 .... $14.99

Grateful Dead for Ukulele

Now Dead Heads can strum along to 20 of their favorites: Box of Rain • Brokedown Palace • Casey Jones • Friend of the Devil • The Golden Road • Ripple • Sugar Magnolia • Touch of Grey • Truckin' • Uncle John's Band • and more.

00139464 .... $14.99

Bob Marley for Ukulele

Ya mon! 20 Marley favorites: Buffalo Soldier • Could You Be Loved • Exodus • Get Up Stand Up • I Shot the Sheriff • Jamming • Lively Up Yourself • No Woman No Cry • One Love • Redemption Song • Stir It Up • Three Little Birds • and more.

00129925 .... $16.99

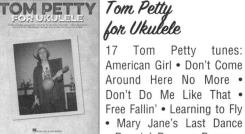

Best of Metallica for Ukulele

18 of Metallica's best arranged for uke: Enter Sandman • Fade to Black • For Whom the Bell Tolls • Master of Puppets • The Memory Remains • Nothing Else Matters • One • Ride the Lightning • Seek & Destroy • The Unforgiven • Until It Sleeps • Welcome Home (Sanitarium) • and more!

02502449 .... $22.99

Tom Petty for Ukulele

17 Tom Petty tunes: American Girl • Don't Come Around Here No More • Don't Do Me Like That • Free Fallin' • Learning to Fly • Mary Jane's Last Dance • Runnin' Down a Dream • Wildflowers • You Don't Know How It Feels • more.

00192241 .... $15.99

Pink Floyd for Ukulele

15 unique arrangements especially for uke for Pink Floyd classics including: Another Brick in the Wall, Part 2 • Brain Damage • Breathe • Comfortably Numb • Have a Cigar • Hey You • Money • Time • Us and Them • Wish You Were Here • and more.

00128556 .... $14.99

Elvis Presley for Ukulele

20 classic hits from The King, expertly arranged for ukulele by Jim Beloff. Includes: All Shook Up • Blue Suede Shoes • Can't Help Falling in Love • Heartbreak Hotel • Hound Dog • Jailhouse Rock • Love Me • Love Me Tender • Suspicious Minds • Teddy Bear • and more.

00701004 .... $16.99

Queen for Ukulele

14 hits from Freddie Mercury and crew for uke. Includes: Another One Bites the Dust • Bohemian Rhapsody • Crazy Little Thing Called Love • Don't Stop Me Now • I Want It All • I Want to Break Free • Killer Queen • Radio Ga Ga • Save Me • The Show Must Go On • Under Pressure • We Are the Champions • We Will Rock You • You're My Best Friend.

00218304.............................. $15.99

Olivia Rodrigo – Sour

11 songs in standard GCEA uke tuning from Olivia Rodrigo's breakthrough debut album: Brutal • Deja Vu • Drivers License • Enough for You • Favorite Crime • Good 4 U • Happier • Hope Ur OK • Jealousy, Jealousy • 1 Step Forward, 3 Steps Back • Traitor.

00371695.............................. $16.99

Jake Shimabukuro – Peace Love Ukulele

Deemed "the Hendrix of the ukulele," Hawaii native Jake Shimabukuro is a uke virtuoso whose music has revolutionized the world's perception of this tiny instrument. Songs include: Bohemian Rhapsody • Boy Meets Girl • Hallelujah • and more.

00702516.............................. $19.99

Taylor Swift Ukulele Collection

Now Swifties can strum along to 27 songs on the uke: Blank Space • Cardigan • I Knew You Were Trouble • Love Story • Lover • Mean • Shake It Off • Today Was a Fairytale • Willow • You Belong with Me • and more.

00365317.............................. $22.99

Order these and more ukulele songbooks at **halleonard.com**

Prices, contents and availability subject to change without notice.